RALIA
THE SUGAR GIRL

KOLA ONADIPE

All rights reserved.

ISBN:978-1-957076-27-0

CONTENTS

1	The Girl Ralia	1
2	Ralia and the Little Bird	3
3	A Hut in the Bush	5
4	Ralia sings a Song	7
5	A Fearful Dream	10
6	Escape from the Hut	13
7	Ralia meets Asiba	15
8	The Villagers look for Sugar Girl	17
9	Ayawa in Apampa Village	20
10	Ralia has an Accident	22
11	The Prince takes care of Ralia	25
12	Ralia returns Home	28

1
THE GIRL RALIA

Her name was Ralia but people called her 'Sugar Girl'. She was poor because her mother and father were very poor. She did not have all the good things which other girls had; but she was happy all the same. She was happy because she was good, and all good people are happy.

She lived with her mother and her father in a bare hut in the out-of-the-way village where she was born. It was a mud hut roofed with thatched leaves. There were many cracks in the walls where lizards played 'hide and seek. Ralia had never gone outside the village. She could neither read nor write, but she was clever. She was pretty too," Young as she was, she looked after the hut for her mother. She could grind pepper, pound yam, look after chickens and gather them at night into their cages. She cooked the meals too. Yet, she was always singing.

Then, a lot of things happened to Sugar Girl.

Ralia! Ralia!! Ralia!!!" her mother called:"Come home, Ralia! I need you. Come home." She shouted again and again. But Ralia was playing with her friends on the sand in the village center. She did not hear her mother.

Again her mother shouted from the door of the hut: 'Ra-li-a! .This time, Ralia heard. She knew her mother's voice. She loved her mother and she obeyed her like a good girl.

Ralia was a little girl of nine. She was skinny, but she had a fine face and a nice voice. She sang beautifully and everyone loved to hear her sing. Whatever she was doing, she was always singing. She did not go to school because her parents were poor; but she knew the right things to do. She was also a kind girl and she had a smile for everyone. For these reasons, all the villagers loved her and called her: 'Sugar Girl'.

Ralia lived with her mother and father in a hut at the edge of the bush in the village of Apampa. She was the only child of her parents.

Her mother was blind. She had lost the use of her eyes when she was ill with smallpox a year after Ralia was born.

At first, it was not easy for Ralia's mother to move about or to cook the meals without seeing what she had to do.

Ralia's father was a farmer. He was strong and kind. When his wife became blind, he did everything he could to make her happy. He fetched water from the stream. He brought firewood from his farm. He went to the market to buy things.

When Ralia grew up and was able to do a few things, she started to help her mother. She did the cooking for her. She fetched water from the stream for her. She helped her to grind pepper. Everything her mother wanted, Ralia did for her.

Ralia's mother was pleased with her. Her father was pleased with her too. They were a happy family. Because Ralia was a good girl and because she had no one to play with at home, her father bought her a dog.

She named the dog: Wara. She loved her dog, and her dog loved her. She cared for her dog like a sister. They slept together and played together. Everywhere that Ralia went, her dog went too. Everything she ate, her dog ate too. She spoke to her dog and her dog understood her.

********************Moral lesson********************

Be happy always. Poverty should not make you feel unhappy. Be hard-working. Help your parents at home. Be good, kind, humble and friendly to everyone like Ralia did.

2
RALIA AND THE LITTLE BIRD

Ralia came home and her mother was pleased. She spoke kindly to Ralia:

"I don't want to stop you from playing with your friends, but you have to go and bring me some firewood from the farm. Take Wara with you and do not be long."

"Mama, but Wara can't go! Have you forgotten that her foot was caught in a trap and she cannot walk?" said Ralia. "I will go alone and come back home quickly. Have no fear about me."

It was late in the afternoon. Ralia took her little cutlass, a rope and a piece of rag. She would use the rope to tie the firewood. She would roll up the rag to put between her head and the bundle of firewood. She would carry the bundle on her head

Ralia left her home singing a song. She met many people on her way. She smiled at them and they greeted her, calling: 'Sugar Girl'.

Soon, she left the village behind and went straight to the farm. It was her father's farm.

But, her father was at home. A few days before, he had fallen from a palm tree and hurt his back.

Ralia took as much firewood as she could carry. She was tying the sticks together with the rope when something dropped from a tree. It fell on her head. Then, a little thing jumped down and stood on the firewood. It was a little bird with beautiful colors, Ralia loved it. It cried again and again as if it were hurt. Ralia pitied it. She wanted to take it and look after it. She put out her hand to pick it up, but the bird hopped forward.

Ralia said: "I don't want to hurt you, little bird, I want to help you."

But the bird did not hear her. Ralia again moved forward to catch the bird. Once again, it flew a few yards and stopped. It cried again and again, and Ralia felt sorry for it. She followed it. Each time the little bird flew a few meters and stopped, Ralia followed it. She loved the little crying bird. "Perhaps, it has lost its mother," Ralia thought.

Ralia did not know that she was going very far from her father's farm. She kept going, following the bird. The bird went on hopping and stopping. Ralia had forgotten that her mother wanted her back home quickly and that she had promised not to be long. She just wanted to help this little bird. "Poor little bird; it is all alone," she said.

At last, the little bird flew a long way and did not stop. Ralia watched it as it went. Soon, she could not see it any more. She stopped. She turned to go back to her father's farm. She looked around and did not know where she was.

She did not know how she had come there or how to go back. "Which way should I turn?" Ralia asked herself.

She turned right and started walking. After a long time, she felt that she was going the wrong way. She turned again. After walking for a while, she found herself where the little bird had left her. Ralia knew that she too was lost.

**********************Moral lesson********************

Always be watchful. Don't take risks. Don't try to get lost. Try to protect your life always.

3
A HUT IN THE BUSH

Ralia was alone, lost in the bush. She was afraid. She called out for help, she had a small voice. Her voice was not good for shouting. It was only good for singing. Again and again she shouted hoping that someone would hear her call. No one heard. No help came.

She threw herself down on the ground and wept. She pulled at her hair and kicked one foot against the other. She sat up, stood up and again threw herself down on the ground.

The bush scratched her body and blood flowed from the scratches.

Ralia thought of her father and mother. She thought of her dog: Wara. What would they do when she did not go home? Her mother was blind. Her father had hurt his back. Her dog had a bad foot and could not walk. Therefore, no one would look for her.

Her mother would only cry and clap her hands, her father would only bite his fingernails and her dog would only bark, and no one would eat that night. There was nobody to make their food. Ralia again started to weep.

She thought about herself. Where would she sleep tonight? All sorts of insects might bite her. She might be bitten by a snake. The wild animals might kill her. She might die and no one would know where she was.

It was getting dark. Once again, Ralia got up and tried to find her way. She threw her hands on her head and as she went, she wept. She did not know where she was going. She Just went on.

After some time, she saw smoke rising from somewhere in front of her. She stopped crying and wiped the tears from her eyes. She ran towards the spot from where the smoke was rising.

Soon, she came to an open space. In front of her was a little thatched hut. The smoke was coming out of this hut. Ralia knew that someone must be living there.

The door of the hut was open. Ralia went quietly to the door and peeped in. It was very dark inside. All she saw was a fire burning, with a pot on it. She heard someone shout from somewhere behind her:

"What do you want here?"

Ralia shook with fear. She turned round and saw an old woman who was carrying a bundle of firewood on her shoulder. She was very old. She was bent. Her hair was gray and dirty. She was very thin. Her eyes were red and her fingernails were very long. She had lost all her teeth but for two long ones, one on each side of her mouth.

"What do you want here?" asked the old woman again

*********************Moral lesson*********************

If people care for you, you also show care for them. Always think of how your parents would feel if they should miss you, when you are lost.

4
RALIA SINGS A SONG

"I am only a little girl. Do not hurt me!" cried Ralia. "My mother is blind. My father has hurt his back. My dog is lame."

"Are you looking for your blind mother or your lame dog here? How did you find your way here?" the old woman asked unkindly.

"I didn't mean to come here. I lost my way in the bush. Can you help me find my way back home?" answered Ralia.

The old woman gave a wicked laugh. "I don't help people. I don't even want to see them. I like to harm them. Don't look for help here. I may even kill you tonight," said the old woman.

"What are you? Are you a witch? Please don't eat me! I am a little girl. Let me go back to my blind mother." Ralia was in tears.

"Who tells you I am a witch? O yes! I am a witch! You see my long nails? They will dig out your eyes, you see my teeth? They will suck out your blood.So saying, the witch pushed Ralia into the dark hut.

Ralia almost fell trying to run, She knelt down and begged the witch not to harm her. But the witch did not listen.

"Be quiet or else I will hit you on the head with this ...," she shouted. She held a long piece of bone in her hand. Ralia thought the bone looked like a child's leg bone.

Ralia was afraid. She ran out of the hut. Before she had gone a few meters, the old woman caught her by the arm.How the old woman caught her by the arm, Ralia did not know. How could such an old woman run so fast? Perhaps she flew like a witch, but Ralia could see no wings. The old woman's nails dug into Ralia's arm and hurt her.

"Please in the name of God, let me go. li you will not let me go, don't kill me. I'll be your servant," begged Ralia.

The old woman pulled Ralia into the hut and threw her down on the ground. Ralia did not

get up. She just lay there. She was sad and tired.

Then, Ralia remembered a song which she used to sing at home. She sang not because she was happy, but because she was sad. As she sang, tears flooded her eyes:

"If you go to the river, don't swim:

It can carry you away;

If you go to the market, don't throw a stone:

It can hit your mother;

If you go on a journey, don't forget home:

Those at home will be waiting;

If you go to the bush, keep your eyes open:

It is easy to lose your way:

If you don't know where you are going

You should know where you are coming from

Because Ralia was weeping at the same time, her voice was not very clean. But, the old woman listened. She had never heard such a sweet voice like that before. She left what she was doing and came to where Ralia was lying.

Ralia did not even see her; she just kept singing her song again and again

The old woman knelt down beside Ralia.

"What a pleasing voice she has got!" the old woman thought. "It would be wrong to do her any harm. I will keep her with me so that she can sing to me all the time." The old woman lifted Ralia up and wiped the tears from her face. Ralia was surprised. She did not understand.

"How can this wicked woman do this?" she thought.

But the old woman patted her on the head. "Have no fear, my child," she said. "I will not harm you. You are like an angel. You will live with me as my child."

Ralia did not know whether to be sad or happy. She did not wish to be the child of this ugly and dirty old woman, alone in the bush. She wanted to go back to her mother. But, she was happy to know that no harm would come to her.

********************Moral lesson********************

Learn to make people happy, Sing for them if you make people happy, they will not do you any harm. Be nice to all you meet in life like Ralia did.

5
A FEARFUL DREAM

The old woman went on talking:I feel like a mother again. I shall tell you my story and you will know how I came to live here a long time ago. I was not always bad. I was married like other women. I was very pretty when I was young." She stopped.

"You don't believe that I was pretty. I can see it in your face," she began, as if she knew Ralia's thoughts. "I was pretty. Sadness and a hard life have made me old and ugly, but I am not as old as I look. I had seven children and I lived with my husband in the village of Apampa.

I know you come from Apampa and that is why I did not like you at first. In less than three years, all my seven children died. My husband ran away from me. While he was running away, he was killed by lightning.

Soon after, all the village people came to my house; men and women, young and old. They carried sticks and stones. They said that I was a witch and that I had killed my children and husband. They drove me out of the house and out of the village. They threw stones and sticks at me.

I was badly hurt. I do not know why I did not die. But, I was very ill for a long time. I had nowhere to go and I was alone. I lived in the shade of that big tree there before I built this hut. Every day, morning and night, I wept. I wanted to die, but death did not come.

I have lived here since then in the sun and the rain. I have suffered very much. Because of all this, I hate everyone from Apampa. I want to kill all of them in that village, if I can." The old woman's voice was very angry:

"I have lived here all alone and I have spoken to very few people since then. I do a bit of farming. That is how I get my food to eat. I set traps which catch all sorts of animals and birds. You can see their bones in that corner.

Once in a while, I go to the market. It is a long walk from here. In the market, I buy all the things I cannot get from my farm, i don't have visitors. The only person who comes here is the wife of a farmer whose hut is not very far away.

She comes in when she pleases; sometimes during the day, sometimes at night. But, I won't go to their hut."

The old woman stopped talking for a while. Then she continued:

'That is my story, my child. Have no fear because no harm will come to you. Let me get you something to eat. You must be tired and hungry."

The old woman stood up and went to the fireside. She made up the fire again and began cooking.

Ralia watched and wondered what the old woman was cooking.

"If it is meat," Ralia told herself, "I will not eat it because it may be poisoned."

For some time Ralia thought of her home and how sad everybody must be now. She began to weep, but quickly stopped herself. She feared that the old woman might change her mind about her if she wept again.

Soon, Ralia fell asleep. She was too tired and too weak to keep awake any longer. When she had slept for a long time, she dreamt that the old woman held a big knife in her hand and was about to cut her throat. She was so afraid that she cried out and jumped up. She was shaking with fear.

Ralia looked round the hut and saw the old woman sitting in a corner with another woman. There were two big clay plates and a calabash of water between them. Ralia knew that they had just eaten a meal and were now resting. The old woman wasn't holding a knife. 1. woman

There were two big clay plates and a calabar of water between them. Ralia knew that they had just eaten a meal and were now resting. The old woman wasn't holding a knife.

The old woman and her visitor were surprised. They stopped talking and looked at Ralia. They did not know why she shouted in her sleep, and jumped up. But they thought that she must have been dreaming.

Ralia moved near them. She knelt down in front of them and begged: "Please don't kill me. I am a good girl. I'll be your servant." The old woman did not laugh. She was full of pity for the little girl.

"Don't be afraid," she said. "I will give you something to eat now, and then you will sing for us." The old woman got up and spooned something dark from the black cooking pot onto a clay plate. She gave it to Ralia. It was very hot and smelled bad. Ralia touched part of it. Then, she quickly drew her hand away.

She began to sing. She sang one song after another. Singing made her happy. At last, she stopped singing and lay down to sleep. But sleep did not come. She wanted to see what was going on around her. She feared another bad dream and she still did not like the old woman. But, she pretended to sleep.

*********************Moral lesson*********************

Always listen to stories by old people: you can learn a lot from them. Be cheerful always by singing happily. Dreams can be very important to you.

6
ESCAPE FROM THE HUT

Ralia lay there quietly with her eyes and ears wide open. There was only a weak light in the hut. The two women could not see Ralia's face, but she could see theirs. She did not hear everything the old women said because they spoke softly. Only a few words came to her.

The two women talked for a long time and Ralia kept her eyes on them. They did not move. Ralia began to feel sleepy, but she tried to stay awake. Then, Ralia saw something which terrified her. While the two women were still talking. The visitor brought out a long knife from her bag. The knife was shining and Ralia knew it must be very sharp. The knife looked like the one in her dream.

Ralia believed that the women were going to cut her throat. The visitor looked towards where she lay and smiled. She did not know that Ralia's eyes were open. Then, the old woman said something. Ralia heard only the two words.

'Tomorrow morning'.

"These women are going to kill me tomorrow morning," Ralia told herself. She started to think of what to do and how to escape. But she was only a little girl. She did not know what to do. She just lay there shivering.

Soon, the two women lay down to sleep. They put out the lamp and lay down on the mat. Ralia sat up so as to hear if anyone was moving. There was no sound. No one was moving. No one was talking.

Soon, the two women were snoring loudly. Ralia did not like this but what could she do?

Ralia lay awake. Sleep did not come. For a long time she lay there as if she were dead. The two women slept and snored.

Ralia thought that dawn must be near. She must escape from this place before the women wake up and cuts her throat. She stood up quietly, opened the door very softly, and walked out into the open.

She ran, She could not see well and she fell down many times. Poor little girl! As she ran, she wept. She did not know where she was going. She did not care where she went. She only wanted to be sure that the two women did not catch her.

To make things worse for Ralia, the sky became cloudy. A strong wind began to blow.

Soon, it was raining. The rain was so heavy, it almost blinded her. She could not see more than a few feet in front of her. She stopped running, and stood still.

The rain poured down on her. She stood shivering. She could weep no more, because she had already cried too much. She fell to the ground.

She had not been sitting for long when she heard a dog barking nearby. The dog was shaking the bush and coming towards her. It was a hunting dog. What would she do? Even if she ran, the dog would catch her.

The dog jumped from the bush. It stood still and barked. It barked like Wara, and Ralia loved it. Then, Ralia looked up and she saw through the bush a hunter pointing a gun at her.

"I am not an animal!" she shouted. The hunter lowered his gun. "What are you doing here?" he asked hunter.

*********************Moral lesson********************

Always try to move away from trouble. You can be lucky to escape from danger, if you try like Ralia is trying to do.

7
RALIA MEETS ASIBA

For some time Ralia could not answer the hunter. She was too terrified to speak. He might have shot her dead. The hunter could not understand how a little girl could be in such a place so early in the morning. Still, Ralia did not speak. She sat there shivering.

The hunter was a kind man. He knew that Ralia needed shelter, food and warmth. So, he did not waste time. He took her hand and pulled her up. Ralia was very weak and cold, but she followed the hunter and his dog.

She was happy that she had found someone who could save her from the two old women. She knew now that someday she would go back home. This man would take her to her family. So they went: the hunter, his dog and ralia The rain had stopped. Soon, they reached a hut.

The hunter knocked on the door, and it was opened by a woman. She was not old and she was not ugly. The hunter's wife was surprised to see a little girl so wet and cold. She did not ask any questions. She quickly took off Ralia's wet clothes and dried her body with a piece of cloth. She gave Ralia another cloth to cover herself up. She made Ralia sit by the fireside to get warm.

The hunter's wife was very sorry for Ralia. She went to wake up her little daughter, Asiba, who was sleeping. When she returned with Asiba, she found Ralia lying on the floor. She was so tired that she had fallen down.

The hunter and his wife did everything they could to wake Ralia up. At last, she opened her eyes. The first person Ralia saw was a little girl who was holding her hand and looking very unhappy. Ralia did not know where she was. It took her some time to remember that she was in the hunter's cottage.

She sat up and looked at the little girl, who was still holding her hand.

"What is your name?" Ralia asked.

"Asiba," answered the other girl.

"My name is Ralia," said Ralia.

They liked each other immediately. The hunter and his wife were happy to see this.

.Ralia and Asiba became very good friends. They played together, ate together, slept together, did everything together. Wherever you found one girl, you found the other.

Ralia taught Asiba many songs and they were soon singing together. Everyday, after their morning food, the two girls went out to the farm and the bush around. They roamed through the bush getting fruit and nestlings Asiba knew how to set traps. She taught Ralia how to do it too. They also spent some of their time helping Asiba's mother.

Now that Ralia was strong, the hunter thought that he should take her home to her parents and her dog. Asiba did not want Ralia to go if she could not go with her.

Then something happened. But, let us first return to Apampa and see what the villagers had been doing all this time.

********************Moral lesson********************

It is nice to be friendly to people. You should find a good friend. The friend can help you and you can help your friend. Both of you can always play together to be happy. Like Ralia and Asiba are doing.

8
THE VILLAGERS LOOK FOR SUGAR GIRL

Ralia's mother waited for her daughter to return from the bush. She waited to hear Ralia's voice as she came home singing. But, Ralia did not come. If Ralia's mother was able to see she could have looked for her. But, she was blind

She spoke to her husband: "Ralia has not come back from your farm. It is getting late. I hope that nothing has happened to her,"

"Ralia is a good girl. She can look after herself, She will soon be home. Don't you worry, She'll be all right," her husband answered,

So they waited. It was growing darker and darker. Ralia's mother called her husband again:"I am afraid something must have happened to Ralia. She can't be so late. Do you still think she is all right?" "No. Now, I am afraid too. Ralia would not stay so long in the bush if something had not happened to her," the father said. Then, Ralia's mother started to weep. She started to talk to herself:

"Ralia, my little girl! So late in the bush!

Perhaps, she has lost her way. Where is Ralia, my daughter, the only daughter I have? What has happened to her? Ralia, the Sugar Girl!" At first, Ralia's mother wept softly. Later, she wept loudly. Then, she went outside and shouted:

"People of Apampa village, don't sleep! Sugar Girl has not come back from the farm!

Help! I am blind. My husband's back is bad. Our dog is lame. And, Ralia is lost!"

The villagers came quickly out of their houses. They listened to the mother's story. The men took their cutlasses, guns and hunting lamps. They followed the bush path that led to the farm where Ralia had gone. As they went, they shouted Ralia's name. No answer came.

All was silent.

Soon, they came to the farm. They looked round and saw the bundle of firewood which Ralia had tied together. They saw her cutlass and the large piece of rag. But, they did not see Ralia.

They looked round again. Perhaps, Ralia had fallen asleep. She was not there. Again and again the men shouted: "Ralia! Ralia!!"

At last, they turned and went home. Ralia's mother was still weeping. Her father was biting his fingernails and her dog was barking.

When they learnt that Ralia had not been found, they were very sad. Ralia's mother cried out, the dog barked louder and her father bit his fingernails deeper. The villagers tried to comfort Ralia's parents. They promised to go again in the morning to look for Sugar Girl.

That night, Ralia's parents did not sleep. They did not speak to each other. Wara too did not sleep. She lay in a corner shaking her tail now and then. Nobody ate that night.

The next morning the villagers, both men and women, went again looking for Ralia. This time, they took their hunting dogs with them.

When they got to the farm, they led the dogs to the place where Ralia had been tying the bundle of firewood. They let the dogs go free. Soon, all the dogs went one way. They barked as they went and the villagers followed.

After walking for a long time, they came to an open space. In the open space, there was a hut. Its door was open. The dogs ran into the hut, barking.

As soon as the dogs went into the hut, an old woman ran out. She was afraid. She did not know why these dogs came into her hut or where they came from.

As she came out, the old woman saw the men and women. She stopped. She looked at the people and she was more afraid. She knew many of them. They were from Apampa. Ten years ago these people had driven her away from Apampa. They had called her a witch; a killer of her husband and children.

She did not know what to do. She just stood there. The people recognised her. They remembered Ayawa, for this was her name.

They remembered all about her. They had thought Ayawa was dead. For ten years, they had heard nothing about her. All the time, the dogs were barking.

The villagers knew that Ralia had been in this place.

"Ayawa," shouted one of the men, "what have you done to Ralia? Have you killed her?" Ayawa was very angry. "Why can't you leave me alone, even here in the bush? You drove me away from your village. What do you want from me now? Who is Ralia?" she cried.

"But you know who Ralia is. She came to your hut yesterday. She is the little girl whom we call: Sugar Girl. Tell us where she is and you will be saved."

"If you don't tell us or give her to us, you will be killed," said another man. "Ralia was here but she is not here now," answered Ayawa. "I don't know where she is.

She left this place before I woke up this morning. That is all I know. You can do whatever you like with me.

One of the village women shouted: "Ayawa, we know what you have done to Sugar Girl!

You have eaten her. But, this is the last time you will kill a child. We are taking you with us to the village. The dogs will eat you up." Then Ayawa answered: "Madia, you have always hated me because I was pretty and you were ugly. I am now as ugly as you. Why do you still fight me? I am ready to die. But know this: I did not do Ralia any harm. She was too sweet a girl; she sang like an angel."

*******************Moral lesson********************

Don't ever get lost. Your parents and friends would worry about you too much. People who like you, will always help you. Don't ever accuse someone falsely, until you get to know the truth.

9
AYAWA IN APAMPA VILLAGE

Ayawa told the villagers about how Ralia came to stay with her for one night. She told them of her songs and how she had left the hut before dawn. But, the villagers did not believe Ayawa. They took her with them to the village.

When Ralia's mother learnt that her little girl had not been found, she was very unhappy.

She wept and wept. She could not eat. She thought Ralia was dead. Ralia's father lay on his back and could not move. He shook his fists and bit his fingernails. Wara crawled and

hollered.

Ayawa was taken to the village chief. The people told the chief what Ayawa had done.

Ayawa said that she did not do Ralia any harm. She told the village chief how she took care of Ralia.

But, no one believed Ayawa. She was locked up. Every morning, she was brought out and made to sit in the village center under the fig tree. Her hands and feet were tied so she would

The village children went every day to the village center to see Ayawa. They called her names. They called her a witch and a killer of children. They danced round Ayawa and sang

"The eyes of a witch, see how red!

The nails of a witch, see how sharp!

The teeth of a witch, see how long!

Ayawa, you can't kill us;

You can't drink our blood, it is bitter, You can't eat our flesh, it is tough.

Mother witch! Dance for us, Mother witch! Fly for us, Mother witch! Cry for us.

The children brought leaves and threw them at Ayawa. They threw sand and stones too. Often, they were driven away by people passing by.

The village chief told Ayawa to tell him what she had done to Ralia. If she did not tell him, she would be stoned to death after fifteen days.

Ayawa was very unhappy. But, she did not weep. She did not even beg to be set free. She just sat there looking at everybody. She did not speak to anyone and she did not care whatever people did to her.

Day after day, Ayawa sat there under the shade of a tree. Every morning, the village chief asked her what she had done to Ralia.

"I did her no harm," was the answer.

Days passed and yet no news came about Ralia. Everyone thought that she would never return. Everyone was counting the days. If not, on the fifteenth day, Ayawa would die.

********************Moral lesson********************

Suffering is part of life. Ayawa suffered for doing nothing. We should not punish people (Like Ayawa) when we do not know whether they have done something wrong

10
RALIA HAS AN ACCIDENT

While all this was going on in Apampa, Ralia was living with Asiba and her parents. Ralia, as we have seen, was now well. She and Asiba were like sisters. They were always laughing or singing or playing games. Asiba's parents were very happy to see the two little girls together.

But soon, Ralia must go home. How would Asiba feel? But, then something happened.

One afternoon, Ralia and Asiba wanted to eat some fruit. So, they went to the bush. They went a long way until they came to a tree with a lot of fruit on it. Asiba could climb a tree, so she went up while Ralia waited below.

Asiba threw a fruit down. Ralia picked it up and dropped it into a bag. While the girls worked, they sang songs and talked to each other. Ralia, who was on the ground, even danced. They were very happy. Suddenly, a horse came galloping round the bend of the path. Ralia was standing on the path and the horse's rider did not see her. When he did see her, it was too late to stop his horse. The horse knocked Ralia down and went over her.

The rider quickly stopped the horse. He jumped down from it and ran to Ralia where she was lying on the ground. Her eyes were shut and blood was flowing from her mouth. Asiba had seen the horse coming, but not in time to call Ralia. She had seen Ralia knocked down and all the fruit in her bag thrown all over the ground. Asiba jumped down from the tree. The rider was kneeling by Ralia. He was trying to lift her, but Ralia looked as if she were dead. Asiba was afraid and sad. She held onto the man and started to beat him.

"You have killed Ralia!" she said as she wept. "You have killed Ralia. You will not go away. You have killed her!"

The young man did not mind what Asiba did to him. He was very worried about Ralia. The poor girl was breathing very slowly and she did not move.

He lifted Ralia up in his arms. He carried her to the horse. Asiba followed him crying.

"Where are you taking Ralia? Is she dead? You can't go. I am going to tell my father. He will fight you and kill you too."

But the man laid Ralia on the horse. He said to Asiba: "Come with us, I am going to look after your friend. She is not dead. She will soon be alright. She will live, Don't cry, little girl. I am not a wicked man. It was an accident." But, Asiba ran into the bush crying. "Don't touch me, killer. Are you going to kill me too! I am going to tell my father. He will fight you, she shouted.am going to tell my father. He will fight you, he shouted.

The young man got on his horse and ro away. He was very sorry for the two little girls.He was sorrier for Ralia. He was sad that Ralia was hurt.

But, he knew that Ralia would not die because the horse had not stepped on her. was only the side of the horse that had knocked her down.

The young man rode slowly. He wiped Ralia's face. But, Ralia did not seem to be getting any better. At last, they reached the town and the horse went straight home. Asiba had run home to her parents. When she was near the hut she shouted: "Papa!

Mama! Come out! A horse has killed Ralia! The rider has run away."

Her father was away from the hut. He was working on his farm. Only her mother was at home and she was grinding cassava. Immediately she heard her daughter's shout, she knew something was wrong.

She ran out of the hut. She saw her daughter running, shouting and weeping. She heard what she was saying and she cried out too.

"Who has done this? Where has he gone to?" she asked.

Asiba was out of breath and could not say much. Her mother did not go back into the hut. She did not even shut the door. She held Asiba by the hand."Show me the way," she said.

She followed Asiba to the place of the accident, but there was nothing to see. The rider, his horse and Ralia had gone. There was no one to tell where they had gone. So, Asiba and her mother returned to the hut. Asiba stayed in the hut while her mother went to fetch her father. He was busy planting yams.

"Ralia has been knocked down by a horse and killed. The rider has taken her away and we do not know where they have gone," the mother cried as she ran towards him.

"This is sad, very sad," said the father. "This is bad news for Ralia's parents. I was hoping to take Ralia home to them tomorrow. Let us go home." They went home. Asiba was still weeping. She told them about the horse and the man who rode it.

"I think I know who he is and where to find him," said her father. "It is Sahib, the good prince. I have seen him coming this way on his horse sometimes. He must have taken ralia to the town. Have no fear, asiba. He is kind and he will look after Ralia well.

**********************Moral lesson*********************

Accidents are part of life. But try to avoid accidents. When accidents happen, help those who are injured immediately. Report the accident to those who can help.

11
THE PRINCE TAKES CARE OF RALIA

When Prince Sahib rode into town, he was very unhappy. He did not even answer the few people who greeted him. He just asked his servants to carry the girl into his house. They obeyed and asked no questions. They saw that the little girl was hurt and that Prince Sahib was sad.

Sahib called for some cold water. He threw the water on Ralia's face. He bathed Ralia's head. He rubbed her feet and hands very hand He rubbed her chest with some sweet smelling oil. He rubbed her face with the same oil. He did not allow anybody to come near her.

Soon, Ralia sneezed. She moved one arm then the other. She moved her legs and opened her eyes. She looked round. The things she saw looked strange.

"Where am I?" she asked.Lie down and keep quiet, answered the prince. "Where is Asiba? Where is my fruit?" Ralia asked.

"Asiba will soon be here. She is on her way here," answered the prince. He knew that Asiba would tell her father about him and her father would come.

"How did I get into this strange place? Whose house is this? I have never seen a place like this before. What am I doing here?" Ralia kept asking questions. "My head is aching. The back of my neck hurts. What is happening to me? I feel thirsty too.Please give me some water to drink." "My dear little girl, you have to lie down quietly. Do not worry. You are quite safe and you are among friends," he said. Sahib called a servant to look after Ralia. The servant helped her to wash. Then, she laid Ralia down on a bed to rest. The room was clean and bright and the bed was soft.

Ralia was given food. Then, Prince Sahib came in. "Eat as much as you like," said the prince. "After that you can lie down like a good girl and sleep."Soon, Ralia was sleeping. She had happy dreams. It was a long time before Ralia woke up. It was already dark. She moved her legs. She opened her eyes. There was a lamp in the room. Then, she rubbed her eyes with one hand.

Someone was holding her other hand. Sitting on the bed was Asiba looking sad and holding her hand! For a short time, Ralia thought she was still dreaming.

"Asiba, is it really you?" she called out.

"Yes, it is I," said Asiba.

Ralia sat up quickly. She threw her arms around Asiba.

"I am happy you have come. The prince said that you would soon come," cried Ralia

"Are you all right, Ralia? Are you really?" Asiba asked. "Yes, I am. I am well again. Nothing very bad happened to me. I only had a cut in my mouth and it does not even hurt me," Ralia answered.

It was Asiba who now put her arms round Ralia. Both of them laughed, wept and laughed. again. They were happy.

When Ralia looked up, she saw Asiba's father smiling at them. Prince Sahib was there too watching the two little girls. "How happy these little ones are!" he said to Asiba's father.

Asiba's father turned to the prince. "I thank you for what you have done for Ralia. I have heard that you are a kind prince. Now I know it," he said.

"Are you the father of these two girls?"

"Ralia is not my daughter; only Asiba is," answered Asiba's father.

He then told Prince Sahib Ralia's story. Ralia is not my daughter; only Asiba is,

He then told Prince Sahib Ralia's story.

"Then, she must be taken to her parents at once," the prince said. "I shall take her myself in the morning."

"That is very kind of you. Now, I can go home. Ralia is safe with you," said Asiba's father.

"Can you not stay for the night?" asked the prince. "It is dark already."

"Oh no! It is never too dark for a hunter. I have my gun with me," answered

Asiba's father.

"Please will you leave Asiba with Ralia?" asked the prince.

Asiba's father agreed to this. He said goodnight to the little girls. Ralia was very happy because Asiba could stay with her. The two little girls sang many songs for the prince. Some made the prince laugh, others almost made him cry.

"Now Ralia, tell me what you want and I will do it for you," said the prince.

"I want to go home. I want to go to my mother, to my father and to my dog," she said.

"Don't you like this place?" asked the prince.

"But this is not my home. It is a beautiful place and you have a lot of things. Still, it is not my home," she answered.

"In that case, I will take you home tomorrow," the prince said.

Ralia was very happy. "Asiba, you must come with me to my home," Ralia said to her friend. Asiba was very happy. The prince sent a message to Asiba's father and he agreed that his daughter could go with Ralia.

********************Moral lesson********************

Always give help to those who have had an accident. Be like the prince, who is doing everything to make Ralia happy after the accident.

12
RALIA RETURNS HOME

That night, Ralia did not sleep. She was thinking of home. Soon, she would be home with her parents and Wara. Everybody would be happy again.

Ralia did not know what to do. She sat up and stood up and even walked about the room in the dark.

At last, it was morning. Ralia quickly dressed herself up. Asiba did the same. At last, the prince came.

"Come along, girls, we are going," he said. The girls jumped up. "Are you sure you know the way to my village?" asked Ralia. "I know it. I have been told. We shall be there in three hours' time," the prince answered.

The girls talked to each other, and the prince. as they went out and were put on the horse. The prince sat behind them. As they went along they sang songs.

At last, they got to Apampa. It was midday. The men and women had gone to their farm. Only little children and very old men and women were in the village. As the horse trotted into the village, dogs began to bark. Little children came out shouting:

"Horse man! Horse man!!"

They were jumping up and down as they followed the horse. The old people came to their doors and looked out. Horse man! Horse man!!" re jumping up and down as they horse. The old people came and looked out.

No one recognized Ralia on the horse for no one thought that she would come back. They all thought that she was dead. In the village center, Ayawa was sitting in the shade of the tree. The horse did not pass through the village center and so Ralia did not see her. The prince jumped down from the horse and helped the two little girls down.

The little children who followed the horse saw Ralia. 'Ralia! Ralia!! Sugar

Girl!" They shouted, singing and dancing. They clapped their hands. Wara too was jumping at Ralia and barking.

Ralia's mother heard the noise. She came out. Because she was blind, she could not see Ralia. But, Ralia ran and put her arms round her mother's neck. "Mama! It is me, Ralia! Your daughter is back home!" she cried. Ralia and her mother were very happy. They both wept, not because they were sad, but because their happiness was too much for them.

"Where is Papa?" Ralia asked. She ran into the hut to her father. He was sitting up. He held Ralia and brought her down to sit on his knee. He looked at her face. He looked at her all over.

He was very happy. The news of Ralia's return traveled very quickly through the village. The villagers came. Even those who were at their farms heard and came. A large crowd gathered in front of Ralia's home. Everybody was happy and everybody wanted to touch Sugar Girl.

All the people wanted to hear her story. They all wanted to greet her new friends. Her mother and father thanked the prince and Asiba. The villagers brought presents to Ralia and to her friend. The whole village was happy. But, happiest of all were Ralia, her mother, her father and her dog, Wara.

When the villagers heard Ralia's story, they ran to the village center where Ayawa sat, tied. Ralia's father thanked Ayawa. He said that if she had not taken the little girl into her hut, Ralia might have been killed by wild animals. The prince took Ayawa away on his horse.

He gave her a hut near the town. He gave her everything she needed. So, once again, Ayawa was free from the village of Apampa. Asiba stayed for some days with Ralia and her parents. Then, she returned to her own home.

But often, Ralia would visit Asiba and Asiba would visit Ralia. The girls would play together and work together, but, best of all, they would sing their songs together.

The prince also was a visitor at Ralia's home.

Perhaps, one day when Ralia has grown up. She will become the prince's wife. But now she is home with her family. Now the village of Apampa has their sugar girl safe again.

********************Moral lesson********************

Be kind, helpful, obedient and friendly to all those you meet in life. Then you will grow up to be a happy child like Ralia. Everybody will like you. Be good. Be happy always and people will like you.

www.ingramcontent.com/pod-product-compliance
Lightning Source LLC
Chambersburg PA
CBHW072138070526
44585CB00016B/1735